bite-sized

Chinese

First published in 2001 by Hamlyn
An imprint of Octopus Publishing Group Ltd
2–4 Heron Quays
London E14 4JP

A CIP catalogue record for this book is available from the British Library

ISBN 0 600 60327 X

Printed and bound in China

10 9 8 7 6 5 4 3 2 1

Notes

Standard level spoon measurements are used in all recipes
1 tablespoon = one 15 ml spoon
1 teaspoon = one 5 ml spoon

Both imperial and metric measurements have been given in all recipes.
Use one set of measurements only and not a mixture of both.

Eggs should be medium unless otherwise stated.

Pepper should be freshly ground black pepper unless otherwise stated.

Fresh herbs should be used unless otherwise stated. If unavailable use dried
herbs as an alternative but halve the quantities stated.

Oven should be preheated to the specified temperature – if using a fan
assisted oven, follow the manufacturer's instructions for adjusting the time
and temperature.

hamlyn

bite-sized
Chinese

contents

Introduction

Chinese cooking is all about harmony and perfection, and is infused with such passion that there is little wonder that it has become one of the most popular cuisines in the world. Nearly every major city across the globe has a Chinatown, as so many Chinese people have emigrated and taken their culinary delights with them.

Cooking is considered an art form in China. Every aspect of creating a meal can be analysed and perfected, and the preparation of ingredients is often considered more important than the actual cooking of the meal. Everything depends on the right choice of ingredients, which must be harmonized in colour, aroma and texture.

This theory can be traced back to the Shang dynasty scholar Yi Yan, who lived sometime before 1000 BC and believed that the five flavours of sweet, sour, bitter, piquant and salty relate to the five major organs in the body (the heart, lungs, spleen/pancreas, liver and kidneys). This theory has developed over the centuries and there is now a widespread belief that eating well has a direct bearing on living well.

It is also worth mentioning the importance of the medicinal values of food. You can be assured that most homemade Chinese dishes are nutritious and healthy (although this cannot always be guaranteed when eating in a Chinese restaurant). Generally speaking, the Chinese prefer light digestible foods and cook them quickly to retain all their essential nutrients.

Chinese cooking lends itself very well to the theme of bite-sized food. An important aspect of Chinese food preparation methods is that all ingredients must be cut into uniform bite-sized pieces. This is for three reasons: first, it agrees with the theory of harmonization, in that all ingredients look similar and there are no visual clashes. Second, it means that the cooking time is minimal – the less time spent cooking, the more time spent engaging with friends. Lastly, bite-sized food is much easier to eat. The use of knives at a Chinese dinner table is considered bad form as generally, only forks and chopsticks are used.

The custom of offering bite-sized morsels has grown over the centuries into an important aspect of the Chinese meal. It is generally known as dim sum, and officially consists of pastry dumplings, rice wheat buns and pancakes filled with meat, seafood or vegetables, but its popularity has grown enormously to include all sorts of wonderful dishes, as can be sampled in this book. Recipes include the traditional Crispy Wontons with Sweet and Sour Sauce (see page 12) and Prawn Toasts with Ham and Sesame Seeds (see page 21) to the more unusual Crab Rolls (see page 28) and Corn Fritters (see page 18). The chapter entitled Little Meals contains some dishes that can be eaten with a fork and others that can be used as accompaniments, such as Bean Sprout Salad (see page 66) and Chicken with Cashew Nuts and Baby Corn (see page 59).

Open your kitchen to the theories of Chinese cooking and enjoy these bite-sized recipes with family and friends!

glossary

Bamboo shoots

These are pale, ivory coloured leaves with a sweet taste. The texture can vary from season to season but is generally crunchy. The leaves are gathered from the bamboo plant at the end of the rainy season and canned.

Black beans

Soya beans preserved by salting and fermenting. Black beans have a strong salty flavour and should always be rinsed before use. They are usually used in small quantities, either crushed or whole, and are widely used in Chinese cooking. Their flavour goes very well with ginger.

Black bean sauce

A thick, black sauce made from black soya beans, this can be used by itself as a savoury dip or used in stir-fries and other dishes. The sauce can easily be made at home by blending a rinsed can of salted black beans with sugar, garlic and soy sauce to taste.

Chinese leaves

Also known as Chinese Cabbage, Pe-tsai and Peking Cabbage, this vegetable originated in eastern Asia several hundred years ago and is best eaten from early autumn to winter. It has pale green leaves, which grow tightly packed to form a long slim cabbage, and a clean, delicate flavour. Use in salads and stir-fries.

Dried wood ears

Otherwise known as cloud ears, black fungus, tree ears or jelly mushrooms, these have a delicate flavour and should be soaked in warm water before use to soften them. Available from Chinese grocery stores.

Five spice powder

A mixture of star anise, fennel seed, cloves, cinnamon and pepper, this spice mixture has a very strong piquant taste so must be used sparingly.

Ginger

Fresh root ginger, often known as green ginger, is very widely used in Chinese cooking. If you are using dried root ginger as a substitute, decrease the quantity as it is much stronger in flavour.

Hoisin sauce

One of the most popular sauces in Chinese cooking, this is used for grilling and barbecuing, and can also be served separately as a dipping sauce. It is made from soya beans, tomato purée and spices and is best known for its use in Chinese barbecued spare rib dishes.

Lotus leaves

The lotus is an aquatic plant related to the waterlily. The leaves are not eaten but used for wrapping food, to which they impart a delicate flavour. Vine leaves can be used as an alternative.

Oyster sauce

Despite being made from extract of oysters and soy sauce, this sauce does not have a fishy taste. It is used widely across southern China and can generally be bought in bottles from supermarkets.

Red bean paste

A sweetened paste made from puréed red beans. It can be dark reddish in colour and very thick and is most widely used as a filling for pancakes.

Rice wine

A wine made from fermented rice, this is very popular in China, both as a drink and in cooking, for its mellow flavour. A dry or medium sherry can be used as an alternative.

Sesame seed oil

Also called sesame oil, this is sold in bottles and widely used in China as a garnish rather than an ingredient.

Shiitake mushrooms

These golden brown caps have an intensely fragrant flavour, but the light coloured stems can be tough and are often discarded. They are used dried as this gives a much stronger flavour.

Light soy sauce

This sauce has a delicate, mildly salty flavour, and is distinctly lighter in colour than traditional dark soy sauce.

Sichuan peppercorns

Also known as Chinese Pepper, Anise Pepper and Fagara, these peppercorns are not actually a pepper variety, but the very fragrant dried berries of a Chinese shrub. They have a strong, distinctive flavour but are not particularly hot.

Star anise

A dried star-shaped pod of a variety of magnolia native to southern China, star anise is one of the spices that are used in five spice powder and widely used as a flavouring in Chinese cooking for its strong aniseed flavour.

Water chestnut

In fact the roots of an aquatic plant, water chestnuts look like white nuts with brown shells. They have a crunchy texture and a sweet taste, but can sometimes be slightly bland. They can be bought fresh or canned.

Wonton wrappers

Made from wheat flour, egg and water, these are yellow in colour. They are available at most Chinese food stores. They freeze well.

Yellow bean sauce

This is made from yellow soya beans and is more of a paste than a sauce. It is sold in bottles and is sometimes used as a substitute for soy sauce, as it is thicker and can produce a richer sauce in cooking.

nibbles

crispy wontons with sweet and sour sauce

potstickers

crispy vegetables with spicy avocado dip

crispy seaweed

mustard-pickled aubergine

corn fritters

deep-fried prawn cutlets in a light crispy batter

crab fritters with water chestnuts

prawn toasts with ham and sesame seeds

Serves 4–6 / **Preparation time** 15 minutes / **Cooking time** about 15 minutes

crispy wontons with sweet and sour sauce

- **500 g (1 lb) wonton wrappers**
- **3 tablespoons light soy sauce**
- **1 tablespoon Chinese rice wine or dry sherry**
- **500 g (1 lb) lean pork, minced**
- **1 teaspoon brown sugar**
- **1 garlic clove, crushed**
- **2.5 cm (1 inch) piece of fresh root ginger, peeled and finely chopped**
- **250 g (8 oz) frozen leaf spinach, thawed**
- **sunflower oil, for deep-frying**
- **Sweet and Sour Sauce (see page 76), to serve**

1 Cut out 5 cm (2 inch) squares from the wonton wrappers. Put the soy sauce, wine or sherry and pork into a bowl and mix well. Add the sugar, garlic and ginger. Squeeze out the excess liquid from the spinach in a clean cloth and add the leaves to the mixture. Combine well.

2 Spoon 1 tablespoon of the mixture on to the centre of each wonton. Dampen the edges and fold to form triangles, pressing the edges together firmly so that the filling does not come out during frying.

3 Heat the oil in a wok or deep-fryer. Fry the wontons, a few at a time, for about 5 minutes until golden. Drain on kitchen paper.

4 Serve the wontons hot with the sweet and sour sauce.

Tip Wonton wrappers, sometimes labelled "dumpling pastries", are sold in small plastic packets in the refrigerator sections of Chinese supermarkets. You can buy both round and square wrappers. They are made from wheat flour, egg and water and are yellowish in colour, unlike spring roll wrappers which are pure white.

Makes 12–16 / **Preparation time** about 30 minutes, plus chilling /
Cooking time about 25 minutes

potstickers

- **12-16 round wonton wrappers**
- **2 tablespoons groundnut oil**
- **400 ml (14 fl oz) hot chicken stock**
- **salt and pepper**
- **soy sauce and/or chilli sauce, to serve**

FILLING

- **8 large raw prawns, peeled**
- **2 spring onions, quartered crossways**
- **1 garlic clove, halved**
- **2.5 cm (1 inch) piece of fresh root ginger, peeled and sliced**
- **1 teaspoon light soy sauce**
- **½ teaspoon rice wine vinegar**
- **pinch of sugar**

Did you know? These little dumplings take their name from the fact that they stick to the pan during cooking. The wonton pastry is first fried, then cooked in stock. The end result is pleasantly chewy and full of flavour.

1 To make the filling, put all the filling ingredients into a food processor, season with salt and pepper to taste and process until finely minced. Turn the mixture into a bowl, cover and chill in the refrigerator for about 30 minutes until firm.

2 Place the wonton wrappers on a work surface. Heap about ½ teaspoon of the filling on each wrapper, placing it slightly off centre. Brush all around the edges of the wrappers with water. Fold the plain side of each wrapper over the mound of filling, making three pleats in it as you go. Press the rounded edges to seal in the filling, then pleat all around the rounded edges to make a crimped finish. There is enough filling to make 12 quite plump dumplings, but if you find them difficult to make with so much filling, use less filling and make 16 dumplings.

3 Heat 1 tablespoon of the oil in a wok until hot. Place half of the potstickers flat-side down in the hot oil and fry, without disturbing, for about 2 minutes until browned on the underside. Pour in half of the stock – this should be enough just to cover the potstickers. Bring to the boil, then lower the heat and simmer for about 10 minutes until the stock has been absorbed. Repeat with the remaining oil, potstickers and stock. Serve hot, with soy sauce and/or chilli sauce for dipping.

crispy vegetables with spicy avocado dip

- **125 g (4 oz) plain flour**
- **pinch of salt**
- **1 teaspoon sunflower oil**
- **150 ml (¼ pint) water**
- **2 egg whites, stiffly whisked**
- **sunflower oil, for deep-frying**
- **500 g (1 lb) mixed vegetables, such as cauliflower or broccoli florets, green beans, whole mushrooms, mangetout and courgette strips**

SPICY AVOCADO DIP

- **1–2 garlic cloves, chopped**
- **4 tomatoes, skinned, deseeded and chopped**
- **1 teaspoon chilli powder**
- **2 avocado pears, peeled and stoned**
- **1 tablespoon chopped coriander**
- **pinch of ground coriander (optional)**

1 To make the dip, place all the ingredients in a food processor and blend to a smooth purée. Spoon into a serving dish and chill until required.

2 To make the batter, sift the flour and salt into a bowl. Gradually beat in the oil and water. Fold in the egg whites.

3 Heat the oil in a wok or frying pan. Dip the vegetables into the batter, then deep-fry them in batches for 2–3 minutes until they are crisp and golden. Make sure the oil comes back to full heat after each batch. Drain the vegetables on kitchen paper and serve with the dip.

Serves 6 / **Preparation time** 15 minutes / **Cooking time** 25–30 minutes

crispy seaweed

- **750 g (1½ lb) spring greens**
- **vegetable oil, for deep-frying**
- **1 tablespoon caster sugar**
- **1 teaspoon salt**

1 Separate the leaves of the spring greens. Wash them well, then pat dry with kitchen paper or a tea towel.

2 Using a very sharp knife, shred the spring greens into the thinnest possible shavings and spread them out on kitchen paper for about 30 minutes, until thoroughly dry.

3 Heat the oil in a wok or deep-fryer. Turn off the heat for 30 seconds and then add a small batch of spring green shavings. Turn up the heat to moderate and deep-fry the greens until they begin to float on the surface of the oil. Take care as they tend to spit while they are cooking.

4 Remove the greens with a slotted spoon and drain on kitchen paper. Cook the remaining greens in batches in the same way. When they are all cooked, transfer to a bowl and sprinkle over the sugar and salt. Toss gently to mix and serve warm or cold.

Serves 8 / **Preparation time** 10 minutes, plus drying / **Cooking time** 10 minutes

mustard-pickled aubergine

- 1 medium aubergine, or 6 small long aubergines
- 750 ml (1¼ pints) water
- 1 tablespoon salt
- cucumber rings, to garnish (optional)

DRESSING

- 1 teaspoon mustard powder
- 3 tablespoons soy sauce
- 3 tablespoons Chinese rice wine or dry sherry
- 4 tablespoons sugar

1 Cut the aubergine into 3 mm (⅛ inch) slices, and cut each slice into quarters. Soak in the water, with the salt added, for 1 hour.

2 To make the dressing, put all the ingredients into a bowl and stir well.

3 Drain the aubergine slices and pat dry with kitchen paper. Arrange them in a glass or ceramic serving bowl and pour the dressing over evenly and slowly. Cover the bowl with clingfilm and chill in the refrigerator for several hours or overnight to let the flavours blend. Serve garnished with cucumber rings, if wished.

Tip Pickles, like this one, are very important in Chinese cooking, as they provide a piquant salty or sour contrast to the other foods at a meal. To make the cucumber rings used as a garnish in this recipe, cut 5 mm (¼ inch) slices from an unpeeled cucumber and remove the seeds. Make a cut in one ring and loop it through another.

Serves 4 / **Preparation time** 15 minutes, plus soaking and chilling

Makes 20 / **Preparation time** 10 minutes / **Cooking time** 15 minutes

corn fritters

- **300 ml (½ pint) vegetable oil**
- **2 spring onions, very finely chopped**
- **1 garlic clove, crushed**
- **1 teaspoon ground coriander**
- **1 teaspoon hot chilli powder**
- **3 eggs, beaten**
- **375 g (12 oz) can corn with peppers, drained thoroughly**
- **salt**

1 Preheat a wok. Add 1 tablespoon of the oil and heat over a moderate heat until hot. Add the spring onions, garlic, coriander and chilli powder and stir-fry for 30 seconds or until softened, taking care not to let the ingredients brown. Tip the contents of the wok into the beaten eggs, add the corn and peppers, and salt to taste. Mix well.

2 Wipe the wok clean with kitchen paper. Pour in the remaining oil and heat until hot, but not smoking. Add level tablespoonfuls of the corn mixture to the hot oil, sliding them in carefully from the edge of the wok, and shallow-fry in batches for about 1 minute for each batch until lightly browned and set on both sides. Lift out with a slotted spoon and drain on kitchen paper while shallow-frying the remaining corn mixture in the same way. Serve hot.

deep-fried prawn cutlets in a light crispy batter

1 Hold each prawn firmly by the tail and remove the shell, leaving the tailpiece intact. Cut the prawns in half lengthways, almost right through, and remove the dark intestinal vein. Flatten the prawns with a light wooden mallet to resemble cutlets. Sprinkle with the Chinese wine or sherry.

2 Dip the cutlets first in the beaten egg, then in the cornflour, and then repeat the process.

3 Heat the oil in a wok or deep-fryer and deep-fry the prawns for 2–3 minutes. Drain thoroughly on kitchen paper.

4 Arrange the prawns on a warmed serving plate and garnish with coriander sprigs, if liked. Serve plain or with sweet soy bean paste.

- **8 large tiger prawns**
- **1 tablespoon Chinese rice wine or dry sherry**
- **1 egg, beaten**
- **2 tablespoons cornflour**
- **vegetable oil, for deep-frying**
- **coriander sprigs, to garnish (optional)**
- **sweet soy bean paste, to serve (optional)**

Serves 2 / **Preparation time** 20 minutes / **Cooking time** 2–3 minutes

Serves 4 / **Preparation time** 30 minutes / **Cooking time** 15–20 minutes

crab fritters with water chestnuts

- **375 g (12 oz) crab meat, finely chopped**
- **50 g (2 oz) pork fat, minced**
- **4 water chestnuts, peeled and finely chopped**
- **1 egg white**
- **2 tablespoons cornflour**
- **1 tablespoon Chinese rice or wine or dry sherry**
- **sunflower oil, for deep-frying**
- **salt and pepper**

1 Place the crab meat in a bowl with the pork fat and water chestnuts and blend well. Add the egg white, cornflour and wine or sherry, season with salt and pepper to taste and mix thoroughly.

2 Heat the oil in a wok or deep-fryer. Using a teaspoon, scoop 1 spoonful of the crab mixture at a time and lower it into the hot oil. Fry the crab fritters until they are golden brown, then remove with a slotted spoon and drain on kitchen paper. The crab fritters should be crisp on the outside and tender inside. Serve hot.

Makes 28 / **Preparation time** 20 minutes / **Cooking time** 20–25 minutes

prawn toasts with ham and sesame seeds

- **1 teaspoon Chinese rice wine or dry sherry**
- **1 teaspoon salt**
- **1 egg white**
- **1 teaspoon cornflour**
- **500 g (1 lb) cooked peeled prawns, finely chopped**
- **7 slices of white bread from a large sliced loaf, crusts removed**
- **2 tablespoons sesame seeds**
- **2 tablespoons cooked ham, finely chopped**
- **vegetable oil, for deep-frying**
- **parsley sprigs, to garnish**

1 Place the wine or sherry, salt, egg white and cornflour in a bowl and mix until smooth. Stir in the prawns.

2 Divide the prawn mixture between the bread slices. Sprinkle with the sesame seeds and ham and press the topping firmly into the bread, using the back of a spoon.

3 Heat the oil in a wok or deep-fryer and deep-fry the toasts, a few at a time, prawn-side down. When the edges of the bread turn golden, turn them over and fry until golden brown. Drain the slices of bread on kitchen paper, then cut each one into 4 squares. Arrange on a serving plate, garnish with parsley and serve hot.

bigger bites

duck on skewers

lamb and courgette fritters

green peppers stuffed with pork and ginger

spicy sliced pork in pancakes

crab rolls

sesame prawns

stir-fried prawns with mangetout

deep-fried scallops

mushrooms in oyster sauce

sauté dumplings

duck on skewers

- **4 boneless, skinless duck breasts**

MARINADE

- **2 tablespoons brown sugar**
- **1 teaspoon salt**
- **4 tablespoons soy sauce**
- **1 tablespoon sesame oil**
- **1 cm (½ inch) piece of fresh root ginger, peeled and finely chopped**
- **1 teaspoon sesame seeds**

1 Cut the duck breasts into 32 small pieces. In a large bowl, mix together the ingredients for the marinade, and stir in the pieces of duck. Cover and leave to marinate for 3–4 hours in a cool place, or overnight in the refrigerator. Spoon the marinade over the duck several times so that the pieces become evenly coated.

2 Remove the duck with a slotted spoon and thread on to 8 bamboo skewers or 4 large metal skewers. Place under a preheated, moderately hot grill or on a moderately hot barbecue and cook the small skewers for 8–10 minutes, the large ones for 10–12 minutes. Turn the skewers several times during cooking and baste frequently with the remaining marinade.

3 Serve the duck hot or cold, on or off the skewers.

Tip Filleted duck breasts are meaty and tender and convenient for kebabs and barbecues. This recipe makes enough for 8 small or 4 large skewers. If cooking on the larger, metal skewers, remove the pieces of duck after cooking and skewer one or two pieces on to wooden cocktail sticks to serve.

Serves 4 / **Preparation time** 20 minutes, plus marinating / **Cooking time** 8–12 minutes

lamb and courgette fritters

- **2 large courgettes, each cut crossways into 12 rounds**
- **3–4 tablespoons plain flour, seasoned with salt and pepper**
- **2 tablespoons sesame seeds**
- **50 g (2 oz) minced lamb**
- **1 spring onion, finely chopped**
- **1 garlic clove, crushed**
- **about 600 ml (1 pint) groundnut oil, for deep-frying**
- **2 large eggs, beaten**

1 Coat the courgettes thoroughly in the seasoned flour.

2 Put the sesame seeds into a wok and dry-fry over a moderate heat for 1–2 minutes until toasted. Remove from the wok and set aside.

3 Mix the minced lamb with the spring onion, garlic and toasted sesame seeds. Press the mixture on to one side of each courgette round, then coat in more seasoned flour.

4 Heat the oil in a wok until very hot, but not smoking. Dip the courgette rounds into the beaten eggs, a few at a time, then deep-fry, in batches, until golden brown, turning them over once. Lift the fritters out of the oil with a slotted spoon, drain on kitchen paper and keep hot while deep-frying the remainder. Serve immediately.

Makes 24 / **Preparation time** 20 minutes / **Cooking time** about 10 minutes

Serves 4–6 / **Preparation time** 15 minutes / **Cooking time** 30–35 minutes

green peppers stuffed with pork and ginger

1 Heat the oil in a wok or frying pan over a moderate heat. Add the garlic and stir-fry until lightly browned. Reduce the heat, add the ginger and pork and stir-fry for 2 minutes. Add the spring onion, celery and lemon rind. Mix well and stir-fry for another 30 seconds. Allow the mixture to cool slightly.

2 Cut the peppers into quarters and remove the cores and seeds. Divide the pork and ginger mixture between the quarters, pressing it down into each of the cavities.

3 Arrange the pepper quarters in an oiled ovenproof dish. Cook in a preheated oven, 200°C (400°F), Gas Mark 6, for 25 minutes, until tender.

4 Transfer the peppers to a warmed serving dish and serve immediately.

- 1 tablespoon sunflower oil
- 1 garlic clove, crushed
- 2.5 cm (1 inch) piece of fresh root ginger, peeled and finely chopped
- 250 g (8 oz) lean minced pork
- 1 spring onion, chopped
- 1 celery stick, finely chopped
- grated rind of 1 lemon
- 4 green peppers

spicy sliced pork in pancakes

- **125 ml (4 fl oz) groundnut oil**
- **2 teaspoons grated fresh root ginger**
- **2 garlic cloves, crushed**
- **750 g (1½ lb) pork fillet, trimmed of fat and cut into fine shreds**
- **2 tablespoons Chinese rice wine or dry sherry**
- **2 teaspoons sugar**
- **125 ml (4 fl oz) light soy sauce**
- **1 teaspoon pepper**
- **1 quantity of Mandarin pancakes (can be bought in most supermarkets)**
- **sliced spring onions and Chinese bean paste, to serve**

1 Heat the oil in a wok or heavy frying pan and fry the ginger and garlic over a moderate heat until softened, about 2 minutes. Add the pork, increase the heat to high and stir the mixture until the pork is brown.

2 Add the wine or sherry, sugar, soy sauce and pepper and continue cooking over a moderate heat until the liquid is absorbed and the pork is dark brown and tender.

3 Meanwhile warm the pancakes according to the packet instructions. When they have been heated through, peel them apart and stack on a warm plate in a low oven until you are ready to serve.

4 To eat, spread a dab of bean paste on each pancake, then add 1–2 spring onion slices and a spoonful of pork. Roll up the pancake and eat it with your fingers.

Variation To simplify this dish, you can cook the pork in advance and reheat it when you are ready to serve.

Serves 8 as a first course / **Preparation time** 30–40 minutes, plus resting / **Cooking time** 45–50 minutes

crab rolls

- 1 tablespoon plain flour
- 1 tablespoon water
- vegetable oil, for deep-frying

WRAPPERS
- 4 tablespoons plain flour
- ½ teaspoon salt
- 4 tablespoons water
- 4 eggs, beaten

FILLING
- 2 tablespoons vegetable oil
- 1 egg, beaten
- 1 spring onion, shredded
- 300 g (10 oz) crab meat, flaked
- 1 tablespoon Chinese rice wine or dry sherry
- 1 tablespoon cornflour
- 3 tablespoons water
- salt and pepper

1 To make the wrappers, sift the flour and salt into a bowl, then gradually beat in the water and eggs to form a smooth batter. Place a small lightly oiled frying pan over moderate heat and pour in 4 tablespoons of batter, rotating it until the base is covered. Cook until the edges curl then flip over and cook the other side. Cook all the wrappers in this way.

2 To make the filling, heat the oil in a wok. Add the egg, spring onion and crab meat. Stir-fry for a few seconds, then add the wine or sherry and salt and pepper. Blend the cornflour with the water and add to the pan, stirring until thickened. Remove from the heat and leave to cool.

3 Blend the flour with the water to make a paste. Place 2 tablespoons of the filling on half of each wrapper. Fold over the other half and then fold the right side in towards the left, and the left side in towards the right. Roll up and seal with the flour paste.

4 Heat the vegetable oil and deep-fry the crab rolls, a few at a time, until golden brown all over. Drain on kitchen paper and cut into pieces diagonally. Serve immediately.

Serves 6–8 / **Preparation time** 30 minutes / **Cooking time** 10 minutes

Makes 12 / **Preparation time** 15–20 minutes / **Cooking time** about 10 minutes

sesame prawns

- **12 raw tiger prawns**
- **2 tablespoons plain flour**
- **1 large egg**
- **2 tablespoons sesame seeds**
- **about 600 ml (1 pint) vegetable oil, for deep-frying**
- **salt and pepper**
- **flat leaf parsley, to garnish**
- **soy sauce, for dipping**

Tip Splitting and pressing the prawns before cooking is not essential, but it does help prevent them from shrivelling up during deep-frying.

1 Peel the prawns and remove the heads, keeping the tails in place. Remove the black veins. Rinse the prawns under cold running water, then pat dry thoroughly. With a sharp pointed knife, slit the prawns along their undersides. Open them out carefully, place cut-side down on a board, and press firmly on their backs to flatten them slightly.

2 Spread the flour on a work surface, add the prawns and turn to coat in the flour. Beat the egg in a bowl with the sesame seeds and salt and pepper to taste.

3 Heat the oil in a wok. Holding the prawns by their tails, dip them one at a time into the egg mixture, then immediately drop them into the hot oil. Deep-fry for 1–2 minutes or until crisp and light golden, then lift out with a slotted spoon and place on kitchen paper to drain. Keep hot while deep-frying the remaining prawns in the same way. Serve at once, garnished with parsley, and with a bowl of soy sauce for dipping.

stir-fried prawns with mangetout

- **500 g (1 lb) large raw prawns**
- **4 tablespoons vegetable oil**
- **3 slices fresh root ginger**
- **2 tablespoons cornflour, plus 1 teaspoon**
- **1 teaspoon salt**
- **1 tablespoon Chinese rice wine or dry sherry**
- **1 egg white**
- **2 garlic cloves, crushed**
- **2 teaspoons black beans, soaked for 1 hour and drained**
- **250 g (8 oz) mangetout, trimmed and cut in half**
- **6 water chestnuts, thinly sliced**
- **½ tablespoon soy sauce**
- **2 tablespoons chicken stock**
- **1 teaspoon sesame oil**

TO GARNISH
- **shredded spring onions**
- **coriander sprigs**

1 Wash the prawns and remove the heads, shells and legs. keep the tails intact. Dry thoroughly on kitchen paper and set aside.

2 Heat the vegetable oil in a wok or large frying pan until it starts to smoke. Add the ginger slices and fry for 30 seconds to flavour the oil. Remove and discard the ginger.

3 In a bowl, mix together 2 tablespoons of the cornflour with the salt, wine or sherry and egg white. Toss the prawns in this mixture until well coated. Add the prawns to the hot oil and stir-fry until they change colour. Remove with a slotted spoon and set aside.

4 Add the crushed garlic, black beans, mangetout and water chestnuts to the wok and stir-fry for 1–2 minutes. Return the prawns to the wok. Mix the 1 teaspoon cornflour with the soy sauce and chicken stock and stir into the prawn mixture until thickened. Add the sesame oil and toss well. Serve immediately, garnished with spring onions and coriander sprigs.

Serves 3–4 / **Preparation time** 10 minutes, plus soaking / **Cooking time** 8–10 minutes

deep-fried scallops

- **12 scallops, fresh, or frozen and thawed**
- **½ teaspoon very finely chopped fresh root ginger**
- **2 spring onions, finely chopped**
- **3 tablespoons self-raising flour**
- **pinch of salt**
- **2 teaspoons Chinese rice wine or dry sherry**
- **1 egg, beaten**
- **vegetable oil, for deep-frying**
- **coriander leaves, to garnish**

1 Cut the scallops in half. If you are using fresh scallops parcook in boiling water for 1 minute; drain thoroughly. Mix the scallops with the ginger and spring onions.

2 Put the flour and salt into a bowl, add the wine or sherry and egg and beat to a smooth batter. Fold in the scallops and toss until evenly coated.

3 Heat the oil in a wok or deep-fryer and deep-fry the scallops for 2–3 minutes until golden brown. Drain well on kitchen paper. Arrange the scallops on a warmed serving dish and garnish with coriander leaves. Serve immediately.

Serves 4 / **Preparation time** 10 minutes / **Cooking time** 10 minutes

Serves 4 / **Preparation time** 10 minutes / **Cooking time** 5 minutes

mushrooms in oyster sauce

- **500 g (1 lb) button mushrooms**
- **3 tablespoons vegetable oil**
- **2 tablespoons oyster sauce**
- **2 teaspoons cornflour**
- **2 tablespoons Chicken and Pork Stock (see page 79)**
- **1 teaspoon sesame oil**
- **finely chopped coriander or flat leaf parsley, to garnish**

1 Brush or wipe the mushrooms, but do not peel them.

2 Heat the vegetable oil in a wok or frying pan and stir-fry the mushrooms for about 1½ minutes, then add the oyster sauce and continue cooking for 1 minute more.

3 Mix the cornflour to a paste with the stock and add this to the mushrooms. When the sauce thickens add the sesame oil and blend well. Transfer to a serving dish, garnish with finely chopped coriander or flat leaf parsley and serve immediately.

Serves 4–6 / **Preparation time** 30 minutes / **Cooking time** 10 minutes

sauté dumplings

1 To make the dough, place the flour in a bowl with the boiling water. Beat well until smooth. Leave to rest for 2–3 minutes. Add the cold water and knead well.

2 To make the filling, mix together the pork, prawns, spring onions, ginger, soy sauce and salt and pepper. Add the watercress and 1 tablespoon of the oil. Blend together well.

3 Roll the dough into a long sausage shape 4 cm (1½ inches) thick. Divide into 3 cm (1¼ inch) lengths. Roll each one flat to make small pancake shapes. Place 1 tablespoon of stuffing on each pancake, then fold in half. Pinch the edges together firmly.

4 Heat a wok and add 3 tablespoons of the oil. Tilt the wok several times until the surface is evenly oiled. Arrange the dumplings evenly over the surface of the pan. Turn the heat to high and shallow-fry for 2–3 minutes to brown the underside of the dumplings.

5 Add 125 ml (4 fl oz) water to the wok and cover. Steam the dumplings over high heat until almost all the water has evaporated. Remove the lid and pour in 1½ teaspoons of hot oil from the side. Reduce the heat and cook until all the liquid has evaporated.

6 Mix together the wine vinegar and soy sauce to make a dipping sauce.

7 Use a fish slice to loosen the dumplings from the wok. Place a large serving dish upside down over the wok and invert the wok so that the dumplings sit on the dish browned side upwards. Serve hot, with the dipping sauce.

- **500 g (1 lb) plain flour**
- **175 ml (6 fl oz) boiling water**
- **125 ml (4 fl oz) cold water**
- **500 g (1 lb) minced pork**
- **500 g (1 lb) peeled prawns, minced**
- **125 g (4 oz) finely chopped spring onions**
- **1 tablespoon shredded fresh root ginger**
- **1 tablespoon light soy sauce**
- **1½ teaspoons salt**
- **1 bunch of watercress, coarsely chopped**
- **5½ tablespoons sunflower oil**
- **pepper**

DIP
- **2 tablespoons wine vinegar**
- **2 tablespoons soy sauce**

a bite more

lamb in lettuce parcels

oriental lamb kebabs

lamb titbits with dipping sauce

chicken wings with oyster sauce and ginger

chicken and mango spring rolls

pork and spring onion pancakes

sweet and spicy spare ribs

sichuan scallops

deep-fried fish parcels

prawns in chilli sauce

special rice wrapped in lotus leaves

stuffed pancakes with sweet bean paste

3)

Serves 4 / **Preparation time** 15 minutes / **Cooking time** about 12 minutes

lamb in lettuce parcels

- **2 tablespoons vegetable oil**
- **½ bunch of spring onions, thinly sliced on the diagonal**
- **1 green chilli, deseeded and finely chopped**
- **2 garlic cloves, crushed**
- **5–15 g (¼–½ oz) dried shiitake mushrooms, soaked in warm water for 20 minutes**
- **250 g (8 oz) lamb fillet, cut into thin strips across the grain**
- **75 g (3 oz) bean sprouts**
- **3 tablespoons soy sauce**
- **about 4 tablespoons hoisin sauce**
- **8 crisp lettuce leaves**
- **mint or basil leaves**
- **pepper**

DIPPING SAUCE

- **125 ml (4 fl oz) soy sauce**
- **2 garlic cloves, crushed**
- **1 teaspoon caster sugar**
- **1 teaspoon lemon juice**

1 First make the dipping sauce. Beat together all the ingredients in a small bowl. Set aside.

2 Heat the oil in a wok over a moderate heat until hot. Add the spring onions, chilli and garlic and stir-fry for 2–3 minutes to flavour the oil. Remove the flavourings with a slotted spoon and drain on kitchen paper.

3 Drain the mushrooms, squeeze dry and chop roughly. Add the lamb to the wok and increase the heat to high. Stir-fry for 3–4 minutes or until browned on all sides. Add the mushrooms and bean sprouts and stir-fry for 2–3 minutes, then return the spring onion mixture to the wok and add the soy sauce. Stir-fry until all the ingredients are evenly combined, then add pepper to taste.

4 Spoon a little hoisin sauce on to each lettuce leaf, place a few mint or basil leaves on top, then a spoonful of the lamb mixture. Roll up the lettuce around the lamb, tucking the ends in. Serve at once, with the dipping sauce handed separately.

oriental lamb kebabs

- 1 teaspoon Sichuan peppercorns or black peppercorns
- 4 tablespoons light soy sauce
- 2 tablespoon Chinese rice wine or dry sherry
- 1 tablespoon finely chopped garlic
- 1 tablespoon finely chopped fresh root ginger
- 2 teaspoons sesame oil
- 1 teaspoon five spice powder
- ¼ teaspoon white pepper
- 1 kg (2 lb) boneless lamb shoulder, trimmed and cut into bite-sized cubes

TO SERVE
- rice
- sweet bean paste (optional)

Tip If you are using bamboo skewers to cook these kebabs, they should be soaked in water for about 1 hour before you use them to prevent them from charring.

1 Place the peppercorns in a small, heavy frying pan and stir over a moderate heat for 3 minutes or until fragrant. Grind in a spice grinder or by hand using a pestle and mortar, and place in a large bowl. Add the soy sauce, wine or sherry, garlic, ginger, sesame oil, five spice powder and pepper and stir to combine. Add the lamb to the marinade, tossing to coat each piece, cover with clingfilm and set aside to marinate for 3 hours at room temperature or overnight in the refrigerator.

2 Lift the lamb out of the marinade and thread on to skewers, leaving a little space between each piece. Reserve the marinade.

3 Arrange the skewers on a rack over a grill pan and grill about 10 cm (4 inches) from the heat for about 8–10 minutes. While the lamb is cooking, turn the skewers so they cook evenly and baste several times with the reserved marinade. Serve with rice and sweet bean paste, if liked.

Serves 6 / **Preparation time** 30 minutes, plus marinating / **Cooking time** about 15 minutes

Serves 6 / **Preparation time** 15–20 minutes / **Cooking time** 40–45 minutes

lamb titbits with dipping sauce

LAMB TITBITS

- **4.5 litres (8 pints) water**
- **1 kg (2 lb) lamb shoulder, trimmed and cut through the bones into bite-sized pieces**
- **4 spring onions, roughly chopped**
- **4 thin slices fresh root ginger, crushed**
- **2 tablespoons Chinese rice wine or dry sherry**
- **2 tablespoons soy sauce**
- **7.5 cm (3 inch) cinnamon stick**
- **1 teaspoon Sichuan peppercorns**
- **2 whole star anise**
- **salt**

DIPPING SAUCE

- **75 ml (3 fl oz) soy sauce**
- **2 tablespoons Chinese rice wine or dry sherry**
- **2 tablespoons Worcestershire sauce**
- **2 tablespoons caster sugar**
- **1 tablespoon finely chopped fresh coriander**
- **2 teaspoons sesame oil**
- **2 teaspoons grated root ginger**
- **1 teaspoon Chinese hot pepper oil**
- **2 garlic cloves, crushed**
- **1 spring onion, green part only, finely chopped**

1 To make the dipping sauce, combine all the ingredients in a bowl and stir until the sugar has dissolved. Divide the sauce between 6 small serving dishes, cover and set aside.

2 Pour 3 litres (5½ pints) of the water into a wok or large saucepan and bring quickly to the boil. Add the lamb and cook for 1 minute. Drain in a colander, then refresh under cold running water, shaking well to remove excess water. Clean the pan.

3 Place the lamb, the remaining water, spring onions, ginger, wine or sherry, soy sauce, cinnamon, peppercorns and star anise in the rinsed pan with salt to taste. Bring the mixture just to the boil over a medium-high heat, then reduce the heat immediately and simmer for 30 minutes until the lamb is tender. Using a skimmer, transfer the lamb to a warmed serving dish. Serve with the dipping sauce.

chicken wings with oyster sauce and ginger

1 Put the chicken wings into a large saucepan with just enough cold water to cover. Bring to the boil, cover and simmer for 10 minutes. Remove the chicken wings from the pan and pour away the water.

2 Return the chicken wings to the pan, add the oyster sauce, soy sauce, stock, salt and sugar. Bring slowly to the boil, cover the pan and simmer for 20 minutes.

3 Sprinkle the chopped ginger, pepper and coarse salt over the chicken. Serve hot, garnished with fine strips of spring onion.

- **500 g (1 lb) chicken wings**
- **3 tablespoons oyster sauce**
- **1 tablespoon soy sauce**
- **300 ml (½ pint) chicken stock**
- **pinch of salt**
- **1 teaspoon brown sugar**
- **2.5 cm (1 inch) piece of fresh root ginger, finely chopped**
- **pinch of black pepper**
- **1 teaspoon coarse salt**
- **finely sliced spring onion, to garnish**

Serves 4 / **Preparation time** 10 minutes / **Cooking time** 40 minutes

chicken and mango spring rolls

- 1 teaspoon grated fresh root ginger
- 4 tablespoons dark soy sauce
- 4 boneless, skinless chicken breasts
- 8 spring roll wrappers
- 1 firm mango, peeled and thinly sliced
- 1 small bunch of coriander, chopped
- 2 teaspoon flour and 2 tablespoons water, mixed to a paste
- vegetable oil, for deep-frying

TO SERVE

- 2 tablespoons sunflower oil
- 2 tablespoons lime juice
- mixed salad leaves
- sweet chilli dipping sauce (see page 79)

1 Mix together the ginger and soy sauce. Baste the chicken breasts with the mixture, then bake in a preheated oven, 190°C (375°F), Gas Mark 5, for 15–20 minutes. When cooked, leave to cool, then slice as finely as possible.

2 Place the spring roll wrappers on a work surface. Divide the chicken, mango slices and coriander between the wrappers leaving a 2.5 cm (1 inch) border around the edge of each wrapper. Brush the border with the flour and water paste, then fold in the two edges, seal again with paste then tightly roll the wrapper to enclose the filling. Repeat the process until you have 8 filled rolls.

3 Heat the oil for deep-frying in a wok, then add the spring rolls, 2 at a time, and cook until golden brown. Drain on kitchen paper.

4 To serve, combine the oil and lime juice. Put the salad leaves into a bowl and toss with the oil and lime juice dressing. Arrange the leaves on a serving plate with the hot spring rolls and the sweet chilli sauce on the side.

Serves 4 / **Preparation time** 20 minutes, plus cooling / **Cooking time** 30–35 minutes

pork and spring onion pancakes

- **250 g (8 oz) plain flour**
- **150 ml (¼ pint) boiling water**
- **2 teaspoons sunflower oil**
- **1½ tablespoons sesame oil**
- **sunflower oil, for shallow-frying**

FILLING

- **125 g (4 oz) cooked pork**
- **6 spring onions**
- **1 tablespoon salt**
- **2 tablespoons Chinese rice wine or dry sherry**
- **1 tablespoon sesame oil**

1 Sift the flour into a mixing bowl and make a well in the centre. Mix together the water and oils and gradually stir the liquid into the flour using chopsticks or a wooden spoon. Turn the dough on to a floured work surface and knead until firm. Let the dough rest for 10 minutes.

2 Divide the dough into three pieces and roll each piece into a long, flat oval shape. Working with one oval at a time, divide it into four pieces and roll each one into a pancake, making 12 pancakes in all.

3 Combine the pork and spring onions with the salt, wine or sherry and sesame oil. Sprinkle about 1 tablespoon of this mixture over each pancake. Fold the two long sides of each pancake into the centre and then fold each one in half lengthways. Form into a round, flat coil and tuck in the end. Roll the coil flat.

4 Heat about 2 tablespoons of oil in a frying pan set over a moderate heat. Fry a pancake for about 5 minutes, turning it once, until browned on both sides. Remove the pancake from the pan and keep warm while frying the remainder, adding more oil to the pan as necessary. Serve hot.

Makes 12 / **Preparation time** 20 minutes, plus resting / **Cooking time** 1 hour

Serves 4 / **Preparation time** 10 minutes / **Cooking time** about 1 hour

sweet and spicy spare ribs

- **1 garlic clove**
- **1 star anise**
- **2.5 cm (1 inch) piece of fresh root ginger, peeled and roughly chopped**
- **2 tablespoons clear honey**
- **2 tablespoons sugar**
- **2 tablespoons chilli sauce**
- **2 tablespoons soy sauce**
- **about 1 kg (2 lb) pork spare ribs**
- **150 ml (¼ pint) orange juice**

1 Crush the garlic, star anise and ginger using a pestle and mortar, then mix with the honey, sugar, chilli sauce and soy sauce.

2 Put the spare ribs into a roasting tin or ovenproof dish and brush them with the sweet and spicy mixture until they are evenly coated. Roast the spare ribs in a preheated oven, 190°C (375°F), Gas Mark 5, for 30 minutes.

3 Pour half of the orange juice over the ribs and stir to mix it with the cooking juices. Turn the ribs over so that the browned sides face downwards. Return to the oven for a further 20 minutes.

4 Repeat with the remaining orange juice, mixed with a little water if the ribs are very sticky and brown at this stage. Lower the oven temperature to 150°C (300°F), Gas Mark 2 and roast for a further 10 minutes or until the ribs are well browned.

Tip Make sure you buy Chinese-style spare ribs rather than spare rib chops. They are widely available at supermarkets and butchers' shops.

sichuan scallops

- **2 tablespoons vegetable oil**
- **750 g (1½ lb) scallops**
- **2 garlic cloves, crushed**
- **1 dried red chilli, finely chopped**
- **½ teaspoon five spice powder**
- **2.5 cm (1 inch) piece of fresh root ginger, peeled and finely shredded**
- **2 tablespoons Chinese rice wine or dry sherry**
- **2 tablespoons dark soy sauce**
- **3 tablespoons water**
- **6 spring onions, diagonally sliced**
- **1 small onion, sliced**
- **1 teaspoon caster sugar**
- **2 shredded spring onions, to garnish**

1   Heat the oil in a wok or heavy-based frying pan until smoking hot. Add the scallops and sear on both sides, then remove and reserve.

2   Add the garlic, chilli, five spice powder and ginger and stir-fry for 1 minute. Add the wine or sherry, soy sauce, water, spring onions, onion and caster sugar and stir-fry for 1 minute, then return the scallops to the wok and stir-fry them in the sauce for 2 minutes; no longer or they will become tough.

3   Arrange the scallops with their sauce on a warmed serving dish and garnish with the shredded spring onions.

Tip The scallop is a very tender piece of seafood and needs only to be shown to the heat of the wok for an instant in order to sear the outside. Never overcook scallops.

Serves 4 / **Preparation time** 10 minutes / **Cooking time** 20-25 minutes

Serves 4 / **Preparation time** 15 minutes / **Cooking time** 15 minutes

deep-fried fish parcels

- **4 x 125 g (4 oz) fillets of sole or plaice**
- **pinch of salt**
- **2 tablespoons Chinese rice wine or dry sherry**
- **1 tablespoon vegetable oil**
- **2 tablespoons shredded spring onions**
- **2 tablespoons shredded fresh root ginger**
- **vegetable oil, for deep-frying**
- **spring onion tassels, to garnish**

1 Cut the fish fillets into 2.5 cm (1 inch) squares. Sprinkle with the salt and toss them in the wine or sherry.

2 Cut out 15 cm (6 inch) squares of greaseproof paper and brush them lightly with the oil. Place a piece of fish on each square of paper and arrange some shredded spring onion and ginger on top. Fold the pieces of paper into envelopes tucking in the flaps firmly to secure them.

3 Heat the oil in a wok or deep saucepan and deep-fry the wrapped fish parcels, in batches, for 3 minutes per batch.

4 Drain the parcels on kitchen paper and arrange them on a warmed serving dish. Garnish with spring onion tassels and serve at once. Each person at the table unwraps their own fish parcels with chopsticks.

Tip Spring onion tassels are a popular Chinese garnish. Trim a 7 cm (3 inch) piece of the green stalk. Reserve the white bulb for another use. Finely shred the top leaves, leaving 2.5 cm (1 inch) attached at the base. Immerse in iced water until the tassel opens out and curls.

prawns in chilli sauce

- **1 tablespoon oil**
- **3 spring onions, chopped**
- **2 teaspoons finely chopped fresh root ginger**
- **250 g (8 oz) cooked peeled prawns**
- **125 g (4 oz) mangetout**
- **½ teaspoon chilli powder**
- **1 teaspoon tomato purée**
- **¼ teaspoon salt**
- **½ teaspoon sugar**
- **1 tablespoon dry sherry**
- **½ teaspoon sesame oil**
- **whole prawns in shells, to garnish**

1 Heat the oil in a wok, add the spring onions and ginger and stir-fry for about 30 seconds. Add the prawns, mangetout, chilli powder, tomato purée, salt, sugar and sherry and stir-fry briskly for 5 minutes.

2 Sprinkle over the sesame oil, then arrange the prawns and their sauce on warmed individual plates. Serve immediately, garnished with whole prawns in their shells.

Did you know? This recipe comes from Sichuan, in the western part of China, where the culinary emphasis is on hot spicy food combined with strongly flavoured vegetables.

Serves 4 / **Preparation time** 10 minutes / **Cooking time** 6–7 minutes

special rice wrapped in lotus leaves

- **8 lotus leaves**
- **175 g (6 oz) long grain rice**
- **1 tablespoon sunflower oil**
- **1 garlic clove, crushed**
- **3 spring onions, chopped**
- **125 g (4 oz) button mushrooms, sliced**
- **50 g (2 oz) cooked ham, diced**
- **125 g (4 oz) cooked chicken, diced**
- **1 tablespoon green peas**
- **50 g (2 oz) canned bamboo shoots, drained and chopped**
- **2 tablespoons light soy sauce**
- **2 tablespoons Chinese rice wine or dry sherry**

1 Soak the lotus leaves in warm water for 30 minutes. Drain thoroughly. Meanwhile, cook the rice.

2 Heat the oil in a wok or a deep frying pan, add the garlic and spring onions and stir-fry for 1 minute. Add all the remaining ingredients and continue cooking for 2 minutes.

3 Cut each lotus leaf into 2–3 pieces and divide the mixture evenly among them. Fold the leaf sections to enclose the filling like a parcel, and secure with string. Place in a steamer and steam vigorously for 15–20 minutes.

4 Pile the parcels on to a warmed serving dish and serve immediately, Everybody opens their own parcels.

Tip Dried lotus leaves are used for wrapping food, but when fresh they can add a distinct flavour to dishes. If you can't buy them, use one vine leaf for each parcel instead.

Serves 4–6 / **Preparation time** 20 minutes, plus soaking / **Cooking time** 30–35 minutes

Serves 4–6 / **Preparation time** 20 minutes / **Cooking time** 15–20 minutes

stuffed pancakes with sweet bean paste

PANCAKE BATTER
- **250 g (8 oz) plain flour**
- **1 egg, beaten**
- **300 ml (½ pint) water**

FILLING
- **6–8 tablespoons sweet red bean paste or dates, finely chopped**
- **vegetable oil, for deep-frying**

Tip Sweet bean paste is a thick soya bean paste sold in cans in Chinese food stores. It is often used as a base for sweet sauces.

1 Put the flour into a large bowl, make a well in the centre and add the egg. Add the water gradually, beating constantly, to make a smooth batter.

2 Lightly oil an 18 cm (7 inch) frying pan and place over a moderate heat. When the pan is very hot, pour in just enough batter to cover the bottom thinly, tilting the pan to spread it evenly. Cook for 30 seconds or until the underside is just firm, then carefully remove from the pan. Repeat with the remaining batter – there should be enough for about 12 pancakes.

3 Divide the sweet red bean paste or dates equally between the pancakes, placing it in the centre of the uncooked side.

4 Fold the bottom edge over the filling, then fold the sides towards the centre, to form an envelope. Brush the edge of the top flap with a little water, fold down and press the edges together firmly to seal.

5 Heat the oil in a deep-fryer and fry the pancakes for 1 minute or until crisp and golden. Remove and drain on kitchen paper. Cut each pancake into 6–8 slices. Serve hot.

little meals

lion's head casserole with garlic

steamed siu mai

chicken with cashew nuts and baby corn

lemon chicken

peking duck

griddled tiger prawns with mint and lemon

pickled green salad with chinese cabbage

bean sprout salad

chinatown salad

special egg-fried rice

chinese leaves with orange dressing

sweet and sour cucumber

chinese leaves with shiitake mushrooms

chinese cabbage and pepper salad

herb dressing

lion's head casserole with garlic

1 In a large bowl, mix the minced pork with the salt, garlic, ginger and 1 tablespoon each of the soy sauce and wine or sherry. Add half of the chopped spring onions. Mix in the cornflour and divide the mixture into balls the size of a walnut.

2 Heat the oil in a wok or deep-fryer and deep-fry the pork balls until golden. Drain well, then place in a clean pan with the remaining soy sauce, wine or sherry and spring onions. Spoon over the stock, cover and simmer for 15–20 minutes.

3 Wash the spinach leaves and cook in just the water clinging to the leaves. When tender, drain well and transfer to a warmed serving dish. Arrange the meatballs on top and garnish with chopped spring onion, if liked. Serve at once.

- **750 g (1½ lb) pork, finely minced**
- **1 teaspoon salt**
- **2 garlic cloves, crushed**
- **2 x 5 cm (2 inch) pieces of fresh root ginger, peeled and chopped**
- **4 tablespoons light soy sauce**
- **3 tablespoons Chinese rice wine or dry sherry**
- **4 spring onions, chopped**
- **1 tablespoon cornflour**
- **vegetable oil, for deep-frying**
- **300 ml (½ pint) beef stock**
- **750 g (1½ lb) spinach**
- **chopped spring onion, to garnish (optional)**

Did you know? This traditional eastern Chinese dish got its name because the meatballs are said to resemble a lion's head. They are usually served with noodles arranged on top to look like a lion's mane.

Serves 4–6 / **Preparation time** 20 minutes / **Cooking time** 25–30 minutes

Serves 4 / **Preparation time** 20 minutes, plus soaking / **Cooking time** 10 minutes

steamed siu mai

- **6 dried shiitake mushrooms**
- **500 g (1 lb) minced pork**
- **5 cm (2 inch) piece canned bamboo shoot, drained and finely chopped**
- **125 g (4 oz) cooked peeled prawns, finely chopped**
- **2 eggs, lightly beaten**
- **½ teaspoon salt**
- **1 spring onion, finely chopped**
- **pinch of white pepper**
- **½ teaspoon sugar**
- **2 tablespoons cornflour**
- **2 tablespoons sunflower oil**
- **1 teaspoon sesame oil**
- **125 g (4 oz) wonton wrappers**

1   Place the dried mushrooms in water and soak for 20 minutes. When they are ready, drain them, remove the stems and chop the caps finely.

2   In a bowl, mix together the pork, bamboo shoot, prawns and eggs. Add the finely chopped mushrooms, salt, spring onion, white pepper, sugar, cornflour and sunflower and sesame oils. Mix well.

3   Place about 1 teaspoon of the mixture in the centre of each wonton wrapper, then pull the edges up and twist to close tightly.

4   Place the wontons in a bamboo steamer set over a wok or a saucepan of boiling water and steam gently for 10 minutes. Serve hot.

chicken with cashew nuts and baby corn

- **3 tablespoons vegetable oil**
- **125 g (4 oz) chicken, skinned and cut into bite-sized pieces**
- **¼ onion, sliced**
- **50 g (2 oz) baby corn, sliced diagonally**
- **50 g (2 oz) cashew nuts**
- **125 ml (4 fl oz) light soy sauce**
- **4 tablespoons chicken stock**
- **4 teaspoons palm sugar or light muscovado sugar**
- **15 g (½ oz) spring onion, sliced diagonally**
- **pepper**
- **1 large red chilli, sliced diagonally, to garnish**

1 Heat the oil in a wok, add the chicken, onion, baby corn and cashew nuts. Stir-fry over a high heat for 3 minutes.

2 Reduce the heat and stir in the soy sauce. Then add the stock, sugar and spring onion and season with pepper. Raise the heat and stir-fry for a further 2 minutes.

3 Turn on to a serving dish or into 2 individual bowls, sprinkle with sliced chilli and serve.

Serves 2 / **Preparation time** 10 minutes / **Cooking time** about 7 minutes

lemon chicken

- **1 egg white**
- **2 teaspoons cornflour**
- **pinch of salt**
- **250 g (8 oz) chicken breast fillets, cut into thin strips**
- **vegetable oil, for shallow-frying**
- **lemon balm sprigs or lemon slices, to garnish**

SAUCE
- **2 teaspoons cornflour**
- **6 tablespoons cold chicken stock or water**
- **finely grated rind of ½ lemon**
- **2 tablespoons lemon juice**
- **1 tablespoon soy sauce**
- **2 teaspoons dry sherry or sherry vinegar**
- **2 teaspoons caster sugar**

1 Lightly beat the egg white in a shallow dish with the cornflour and salt. Add the strips of chicken and turn gently to coat. Set aside.

2 To prepare the sauce, blend the cornflour in a jug with 2 tablespoons of the stock or water to a smooth paste. Add the remaining stock and the remaining sauce ingredients. Stir well to combine.

3 Pour enough oil into a wok to come 2.5–4 cm (1–1½ inches) up the sides. Heat over a moderate heat until hot, but not smoking, then shallow-fry a few strips of chicken for about 2 minutes or until lightly browned. Lift out with a slotted spoon and drain on kitchen paper while shallow-frying the remaining chicken strips.

4 Carefully pour the oil out of the wok. Pour in the sauce mixture and bring to the boil over a high heat, stirring constantly until thickened and glossy. Return the chicken to the wok and stir-fry for 2 minutes or until tender and evenly coated in the lemon sauce. Garnish with lemon balm or lemon slices and serve at once.

Tip This simple recipe originated in Hong Kong. It is delicious served with spinach or broccoli.

Serves 2 / **Preparation time** 10 minutes / **Cooking time** 20 minutes

Serves 4-6 / **Preparation time** 1 hour, plus hanging overnight and 2 hours the following day / **Cooking time** 1½ hours

peking duck

1 Immerse the duck in a saucepan of boiling water for 2 minutes, then drain thoroughly. Hang up the duck to dry in a well-ventilated room overnight.

2 Mix together the soy sauce and sugar, and rub over the duck. Hang for 2 hours until the soy and sugar coating is completely dry. Place the duck on a rack in a roasting tin and cook in a preheated oven, 200°C (400°F), Gas Mark 6, for 1½ hours.

3 Meanwhile, warm the pancakes according to the packet instructions.

4 Cut off all the crispy skin from the duck, cut it into fairly small pieces and arrange them on a warmed serving dish. Garnish with the cucumber matchsticks.

5 Remove all the meat from the duck and arrange it on another warmed serving dish. Garnish with spring onion matchsticks. Place the hoisin sauce in a small bowl.

6 Each guest prepares their own pancakes, spreading a little hoisin sauce over a pancake, covering it with a piece of duck skin and some meat and topping it with a little cucumber and spring onion.

- **2–2.25 kg (4–4½ lb) oven-ready duck**
- **2 tablespoons soy sauce**
- **2 tablespoons dark brown sugar**
- **1 quantity of Mandarin Pancakes – allow 3–4 pancakes per person (can be bought in most supermarkets)**

TO SERVE

- **1 small cucumber, cut into 5 cm (2 inch) matchsticks**
- **1 bunch of spring onions, cut into 5 cm (2 inch) matchsticks**
- **8 tablespoons hoisin sauce**

Serves 4 / **Preparation time** 30 minutes, plus marinating / **Cooking time** 8–12 minutes

griddled tiger prawns with mint and lemon

- **750 g (1½ lb) raw tiger prawns, peeled, heads removed and deveined**
- **1 large bunch of mint, chopped**
- **2 garlic cloves, crushed**
- **8 tablespoons lemon juice**
- **sea salt and pepper**
- **mint leaves, to garnish**

1 Place the prawns in a mixing bowl. Add the mint, garlic and lemon juice, season to taste with salt and pepper and leave to marinate for 3 hours or overnight.

2 Heat a griddle pan. Spoon the prawns and marinade on to the griddle, in batches, and cook for 2–3 minutes on each side. Serve immediately, garnished with mint leaves.

pickled green salad with chinese cabbage

- **500 g (1 lb) cucumber, peeled**
- **500 g (1 lb) Chinese cabbage, cored and chopped**
- **2 teaspoons salt**
- **1 teaspoon garlic, crushed**
- **1 teaspoon Sichuan or black peppercorns, ground**
- **1 teaspoon sugar**
- **1 tablespoon light soy sauce**
- **2 tablespoons sesame oil**
- **1 tablespoon red wine vinegar**

1 Crush the cucumber until cracks appear on the surface. Quarter it lengthways, then cut it into pieces and put it into a bowl. Add the cabbage, sprinkle with salt and leave for 2 hours.

2 Rinse the salt from the vegetables and drain on kitchen paper.

3 Mix together the garlic, pepper, sugar, soy sauce, oil and vinegar. Pour the dressing over the vegetables, mix well and leave to stand for at least 3 hours before serving.

Serves 4–6 / **Preparation time** 15 minutes, plus standing time

bean sprout salad

- **500 g (1 lb) fresh bean sprouts**
- **2.5 litres (4 pints) water**
- **1 teaspoon salt**
- **50 g (2 oz) cooked ham or chicken, thinly sliced**

DRESSING
- **2 tablespoons soy sauce**
- **1 tablespoon vinegar**
- **1 tablespoon sesame oil**

1 Wash the bean sprouts in cold water, discarding the husks and other small pieces that float to the surface (it is not necessary to top and tail each bean sprout).

2 Bring the water, with the salt added, to the boil, and add the bean sprouts. Cook for 2 minutes only. Drain in a colander, rinse under cold water until cool, and drain again.

3 Mix together the ingredients for the dressing. Place the bean sprouts in a serving bowl and pour over the dressing, tossing well to combine. Leave to stand for 10–20 minutes, then serve topped with thinly sliced ham or chicken.

Did you know? Chinese salads are rarely based on raw vegetables. They are usually composed of vegetables which are blanched, refreshed in cold water and mixed in a dressing.

Serves 4 / **Preparation time** 10 minutes, plus standing / **Cooking time** 5 minutes

Serves 4 / **Preparation time** 30 minutes

chinatown salad

- **300 g (10 oz) fresh bean sprouts**
- **125 g (4 oz) mushrooms, thinly sliced**
- **1 bunch of spring onions, chopped**
- **1 chicken breast, cooked and shredded**
- **1 banana, sliced**
- **250 g (8 oz) can sliced peaches, drained, chopped and juice reserved**
- **4 celery sticks, chopped**
- **25 g (1 oz) cashew nuts**
- **celery leaves, to garnish**

DRESSING

- **125 ml (4 fl oz) single cream**
- **2 tablespoons soy sauce**
- **1 tablespoon malt vinegar**
- **1 tablespoon reserved peach juice from the can**
- **salt and pepper**

1 Put the bean sprouts into a bowl with the mushrooms. Add the spring onions, shredded chicken, banana, peaches, celery and nuts.

2 Put all the dressing ingredients into a screw-top jar and shake well. Pour the dressing over the salad and toss all the ingredients together. Garnish with the celery leaves.

3 Serve this salad with ham or cold roast pork and sliced tomatoes sprinkled with basil. Alternatively, slice the meat into thin shreds and stir it into the salad.

Serves 4 / **Preparation time** 10 minutes / **Cooking time** 8–10 minutes

special egg-fried rice

- **2–3 eggs**
- **2 spring onions, finely chopped**
- **2 teaspoons salt**
- **3 tablespoons vegetable oil**
- **125 g (4 oz) cooked peeled prawns**
- **125 g (4 oz) cooked chicken or pork, diced**
- **50 g (2 oz) bamboo shoots, diced**
- **4 tablespoons cooked peas**
- **1 tablespoon light soy sauce**
- **375–500 g (12 oz–1 lb) cold cooked rice**
- **chopped spring onions, to garnish**

1 Break the eggs into a small bowl and add 1 teaspoon of the finely chopped spring onions and a pinch of the salt. Beat lightly together with a fork.

2 Heat about 1 tablespoon of the oil in the wok and add the beaten egg mixture. Stir constantly until the eggs are scrambled and set. Remove the scrambled eggs from the wok and set aside in a bowl.

3 Heat the remaining oil in the wok, and add the prawns, chicken or pork, bamboo shoots, peas and the remaining chopped spring onions. Stir-fry briskly for 1 minute. Add the soy sauce and stir-fry for 2–3 minutes, then add the cooked rice, scrambled eggs and the remaining salt. Stir well to break up the scrambled eggs into small pieces and separate the grains of rice. Serve hot, garnished with spring onions.

chinese leaves with orange dressing

- **1 head of Chinese leaves, shredded**
- **50 g (2 oz) butter**
- **grated rind and juice of 1 orange**
- **½ teaspoon grated nutmeg**
- **salt**
- **chopped parsley, to garnish**

1 Cook the Chinese leaves in a saucepan with a little boiling lightly salted water for 5 minutes. Drain well in a colander.

2 Put the butter, orange rind and juice, and nutmeg into the pan. Add the Chinese leaves and toss well.

3 Transfer to a warmed serving dish and serve hot, garnished with parsley.

Serves 6 / **Preparation time** 10 minutes / **Cooking time** 5 minutes

Serves 4 / **Preparation time** 5 minutes / **Cooking time** 5 minutes

sweet and sour cucumber

- **1 cucumber**
- **1 tablespoon vegetable oil**
- **2 tablespoons white wine vinegar or cider vinegar**
- **2 tablespoons caster sugar**
- **salt**

1 Cut off the ends of the cucumber and discard, then cut the cucumber crossways into 6 equal pieces. Cut each piece of cucumber lengthways into eighths, then cut out the seeds and discard them.

2 Heat a wok until hot. Add the oil and swirl it over a moderate heat until hot. Add the wine or cider vinegar and the sugar and stir until sizzling, then add the cucumber strips and salt to taste. Stir-fry for 2–3 minutes or until the cucumber is softened but still crunchy. Serve at once.

Tip This simple vegetable dish is good with rich-tasting meat dishes because it is sharp and cool in flavour. It also goes well with fish.

Serves 4 / **Preparation time** 10 minutes / **Cooking time** 5–10 minutes

chinese leaves with shiitake mushrooms

- **375 g (12 oz) Chinese leaves**
- **125 g (4 oz) shiitake mushrooms, thinly sliced**
- **1 cm (½ inch) piece of fresh root ginger, peeled and finely shredded**
- **1 garlic clove, crushed**
- **½ tablespoon light soy sauce**
- **2 teaspoons soft light brown sugar**
- **1 green chilli, deseeded and finely chopped**
- **1 teaspoon sesame oil**
- **3 spring onions, finely chopped**

1 Shred the Chinese leaves into 1 cm (½ inch) strips and place in a large bowl. Mix all the other ingredients in a separate bowl, then add them to the Chinese leaves and toss lightly.

2 Place a large piece of double foil on a work surface, then pile the mixture in the centre. Bring up the edges and press to seal. Cook the foil parcel under a preheated hot grill or on a barbecue over hot coals for 5–10 minutes, gently shaking them occasionally, until the Chinese leaves and mushrooms are tender.

Tip Other varieties of mushrooms, such as brown chestnut mushrooms or oyster mushrooms, may be used instead of shiitakes.

chinese cabbage and pepper salad

- 1 leek, thinly sliced
- 1 Chinese cabbage, shredded
- 1 green pepper, cored, deseeded and thinly sliced
- 6 tablespoons Herb Dressing (see below)

1 Separate the leek slices into rings and mix with the shredded Chinese cabbage in a bowl. Add the green pepper and the dressing and toss thoroughly. Transfer to a salad bowl and serve immediately.

Serves 6–8 / **Preparation time** 10 minutes

herb dressing

- 150 ml (¼ pint) natural yogurt
- 1 garlic clove, crushed
- 1 tablespoon cider vinegar
- 1 teaspoon clear honey
- 15 g (½ oz) flat leaf parsley
- 15 g (½ oz) mixed mint and chives
- salt and pepper

1 Put all the ingredients into a food processor, add salt and pepper to taste, and whizz for 1–2 minutes until well blended. Transfer to a bowl, cover and chill until required.

Makes about 175 ml (6 fl oz) / **Preparation time** 5 minutes

dips and sauces

shantung sauce

sweet and sour sauce

sesame paste sauce

tomato sauce

honey sauce

hot and sour sauce

sweet chilli dipping sauce

chicken and pork stock

Serves 4 / **Preparation time** 5–10 minutes / **Cooking time** 5 minutes

shantung sauce

- 2 garlic cloves, finely chopped
- 2 chillies, finely chopped
- 2 spring onions, finely chopped
- 1 teaspoon sugar
- 1 teaspoon sesame oil
- 1 tablespoon chicken stock
- ½ teaspoon salt
- pinch of monosodium glutamate (optional)
- 1 tablespoon Chinese rice wine or dry sherry
- 2 teaspoons wine vinegar
- ½ tablespoon red chilli oil

1 Heat a wok or frying pan, then add the garlic, chillies, spring onions, sugar and sesame oil. Stir-fry for 1 minute, then add the chicken stock, salt, monosodium glutamate, if using, sherry, vinegar and chilli oil. Stir over a moderate heat until boiling, then simmer briefly until slightly thickened.

Tip This sauce from northern China goes well with chicken and rice dishes.

sweet and sour sauce

- 1 tablespoon sunflower oil
- 2 garlic cloves, crushed
- 2 tablespoons light soy sauce
- 2 tablespoons clear honey
- 2 tablespoons wine vinegar
- 2 tablespoons tomato purée
- 2 teaspoons chilli sauce
- 2 tablespoons Chinese wine
- 2 teaspoons of a thin cornflour and water paste

1 Heat the sunflower oil in a wok and stir-fry the garlic for 1 minute. Add all the remaining ingredients, bring to the boil and cook for 2 minutes.

Serves 4 / **Preparation time** 5 minutes / **Cooking time** 3–4 minutes

Serves 4 / **Preparation time** 5 minutes

sesame paste sauce

- **2 tablespoons sesame seed paste**
- **4 tablespoons water**
- **4 tablespoons chopped spring onions**
- **1 teaspoon crushed garlic**
- **1 tablespoon soy sauce**
- **2 tablespoons red wine vinegar**
- **2 teaspoons hot pepper oil**
- **1 teaspoon salt**

1 In a bowl, mix the sesame seed paste with the water until evenly combined. Blend in the chopped spring onions, garlic, soy sauce, vinegar, hot pepper oil and salt.

tomato sauce

- **1 tablespoon sunflower oil**
- **1 onion, diced**
- **3 canned pineapple rings, diced**
- **1 green pepper, cored, deseeded and diced**
- **3 tablespoons sugar**
- **3 tablespoons wine vinegar**
- **6 tablespoons water**
- **3 tablespoons tomato puree**
- **1 tablespoon Chinese rice wine or dry sherry**
- **2 teaspoons cornflour**
- **a pinch of salt**
- **1 teaspoon sesame oil**

1 Heat the oil in a wok or frying pan.

2 Add the onion, pineapple, and green pepper to the wok and stir-fry for about 30 seconds. Mix together the sugar, vinegar, water, tomato purée, wine, cornflour, salt and sesame oil, and add to the vegetables.

3 Bring to the boil, stirring. If the sauce becomes too thick add a little water.

Tip This versatile sauce from eastern China is excellent poured over simply cooked white fish and may also be used as a dip.

Makes about 150 ml (¼ pint) / **Preparation time** 15 minutes / **Cooking time** about 10 minutes

Makes 100 ml (3½ fl oz) / **Preparation time** 20 minutes /
Cooking time 5 minutes

honey sauce

- **3 tablespoons clear honey**
- **1½ tablespoons sugar**
- **2 teaspoons cornflour**
- **3 tablespoons water**

1 Place all ingredients in a small
saucepan set over a gentle heat
and cook, stirring constantly, until
thickened and smooth.

hot and sour sauce

- **2 tablespoons corn oil**
- **2–3 spring onions,
  finely chopped**
- **2–3 slices of fresh root, ginger,
  finely chopped**
- **1 garlic clove, crushed**
- **2 tablespoons dry sherry**
- **1 teaspoon sugar**
- **2 tablespoons soy sauce**
- **1 tablespoon chilli sauce**
- **2 tablespoons white wine
  vinegar**
- **125 ml (4fl oz) water**

1 Heat the oil in a wok or frying pan.
Add the spring onions, ginger and
garlic and fry for a few seconds.

2 Add the sherry, sugar, soy sauce, chilli
sauce, white wine vinegar and water.
Bring to the boil, reduce the heat and
simmer for 5 minutes.

Makes about 260 ml (8½ fl oz) / **Preparation time** 20 minutes /
Cooking time 5 minutes

Serves 4 / **Preparation time** 5 minutes / **Cooking time** 15 minutes

sweet chilli dipping sauce

- 1 tablespoon olive oil
- 2 shallots, finely chopped
- 2 garlic cloves, crushed
- 250 g (8 oz) canned chopped tomatoes
- 3 tablespoons bottled sweet chilli sauce
- 50 g (2 oz) caster sugar
- 3 tablespoons white wine vinegar
- 3 tablespoons water
- 1 red chilli, deseeded and finely chopped
- 1 carrot, peeled and shredded

1 Heat the oil in a frying pan and fry the shallots and garlic for a few minutes to soften, then add the tomatoes and simmer until the liquid has reduced by half. Remove from the heat and leave to cool. Strain through a sieve and stir in the bottled sweet chilli sauce.

2 Put the sugar, vinegar, water and chilli into a small saucepan and heat gently to dissolve the sugar, then stir in the shredded carrot. Leave to cool, then stir into the tomato mixture.

chicken and pork stock

- 2.75 litres (5 pints) water
- 500 g (1 lb) chicken pieces
- 500 g (1 lb) pork spare ribs

1 Bring the water to the boil in a large saucepan, add the chicken pieces and pork spare ribs, then bring back to the boil and skim off any scum that rises to the surface.

2 Reduce the heat, then partially cover the pan and simmer gently for at least 2 hours or until the liquid is reduced by about one-third. Remove the pan from the heat and leave to cool, then strain through a sieve. When the stock is cold, remove the solid fat from the surface and discard.

Tip This stock, with its subtle flavour, will keep in the refrigerator for about a week, or for about 3 months in the freezer.

Serves 4 / **Preparation time** 5 minutes / **Cooking time** 15 minutes

acknowledgements

Picture credits
Octopus Publishing Group Ltd./Bill Reavell Front Cover bottom left, Back Cover, 1, 3, 6 left, 45, 55, /David Loftus Front Cover bottom right, 7 centre, 9 right, 48, 72, /Ian Wallace Front Cover top, 14, 39, /James Merrell 8 left, /James Murphy 25, 61, 78, /Jean Cazals 4 left, 5 right, 6 centre, 7 left, 7 right, 8 right, 9 centre, 13, 15, 17, 19, 21, 23, 34, 42, 53, 56, 62, 65, /Neil Mersh 6 right, 11, /Paul Williams 5 left, 26, 50, 51, /Philip Webb 4 right, 29, 69, /Roger Stowell 33, 67, /Sandra Lane 8 centre, 9 left, 30, 37, 47, 71, 75, /Sean Myers 59

Editor: Abi Rowsell
Copy editor: Anne Crane
Proofreader: Linda Doeser
Indexer: Hilary Bird
Executive Art Editor: Geoff Fennell
Designer: Louise Griffiths
Production Controller: Jo Sim
Picture researcher: Jennifer Veall